WHY WE LOVE TENNIS

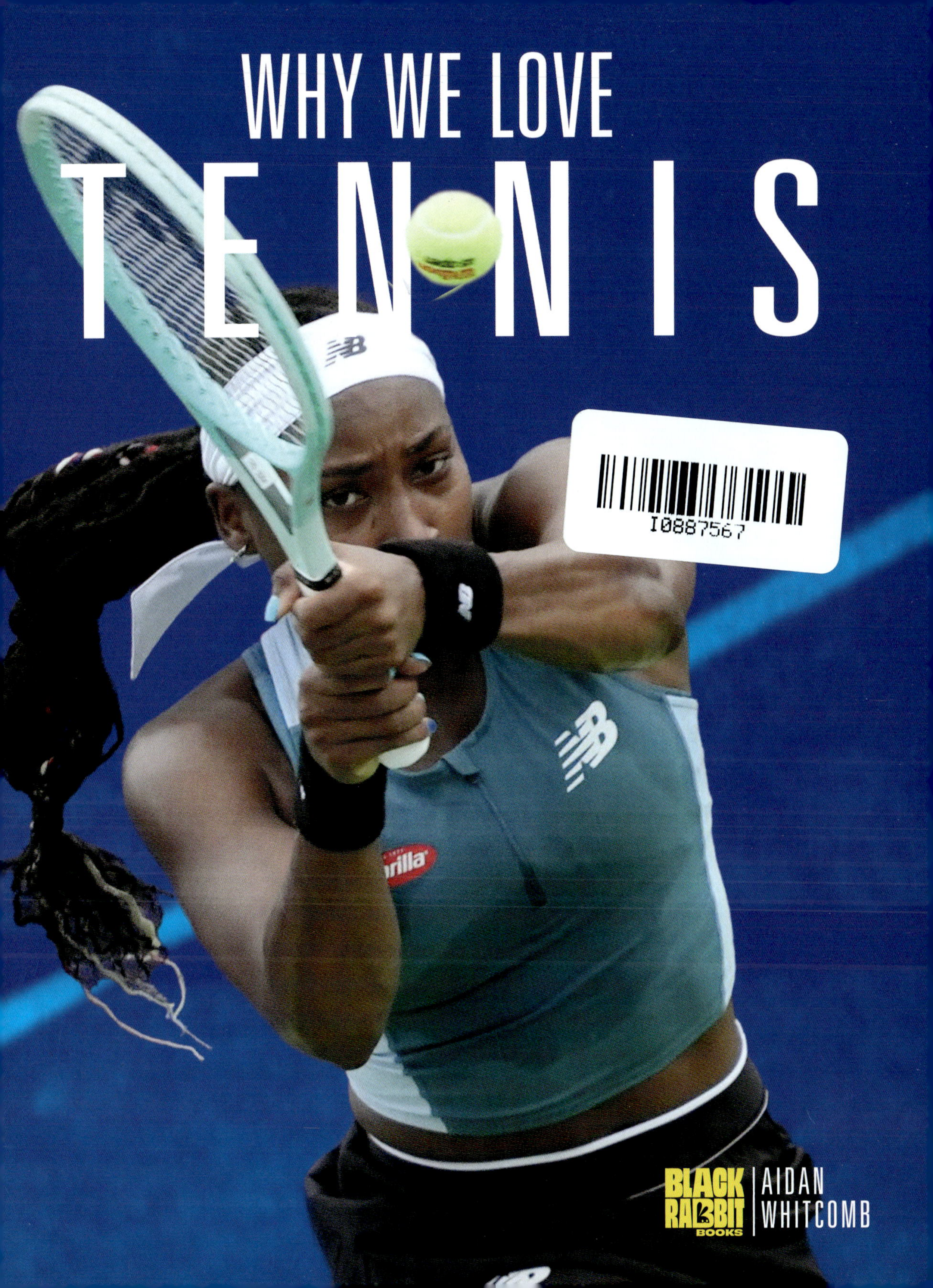

BLACK RABBIT BOOKS

AIDAN WHITCOMB

TABLE OF CONTENTS

1

Birth of Tennis

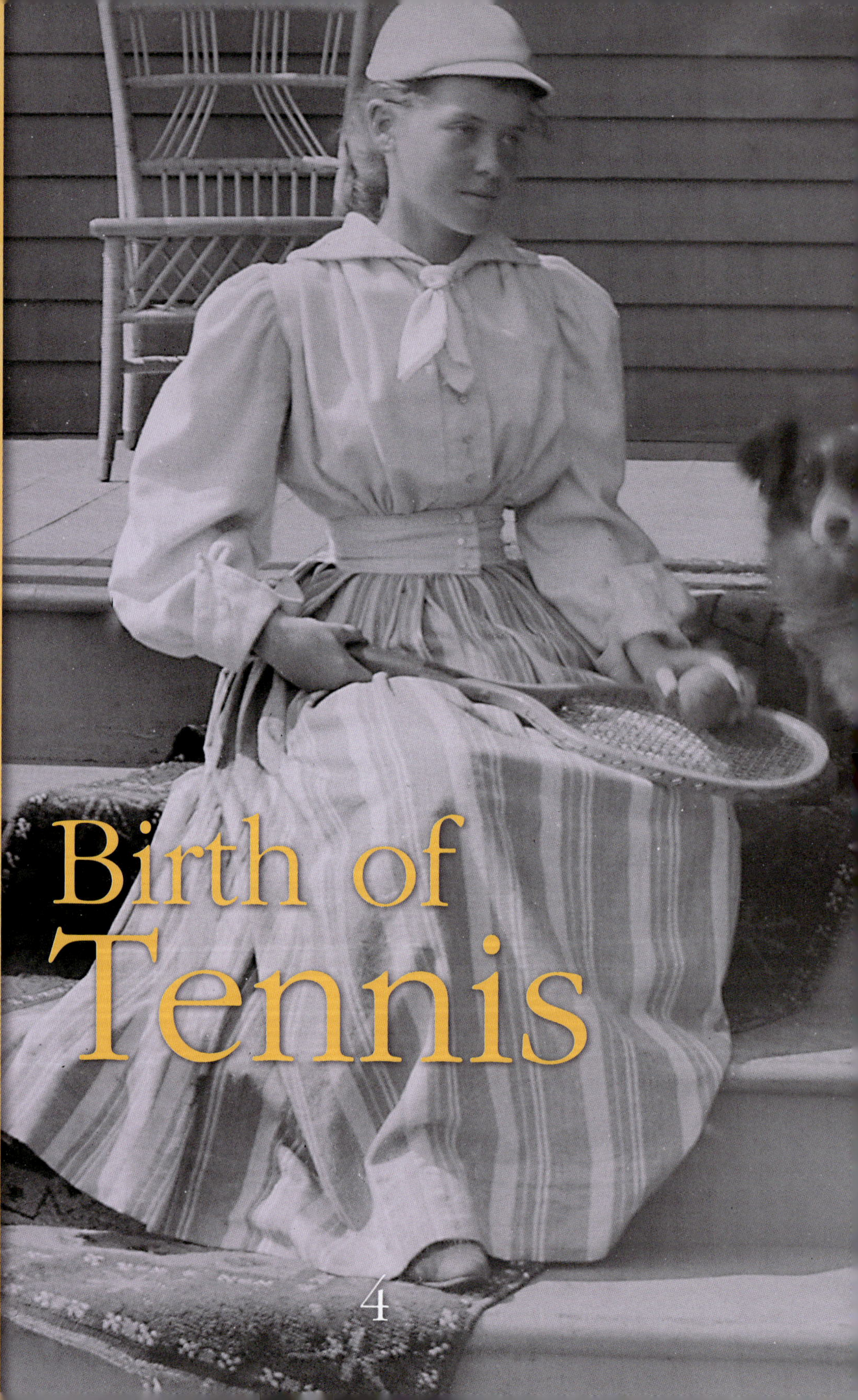

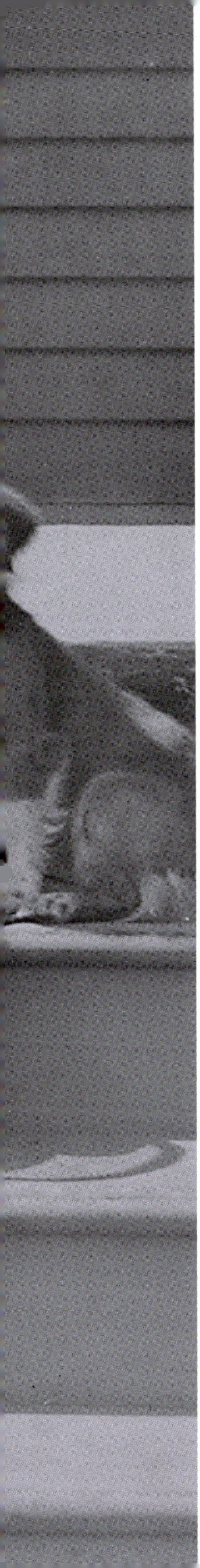

Tennis is an old sport. It started in England. The first book of tennis rules was created in 1873. Soon after that, it spread to the United States. People loved the new sport. Tennis had many fans early on.

Over time, tennis drew in more fans. Today it is the fourth-most watched sport in the world. There are about 1 billion fans! Fans love the exciting shots and rallies.

Did You Know?
More than 23 million Americans have played tennis.

2

Tennis Greats

Billie Jean King

There are many tennis legends. Billie Jean King and Rod Laver were stars in the 1960s and 70s. They were dominant! These players had many fans.

Serena Williams is one of the greatest women's players. She won 85 percent of her career matches! There are many male legends too. Who's the GOAT? Most would say Novak Djokovic. Roger Federer and Rafael Nadal are also very good. Fans called these men the "Big Three."

Think About It

What skills make tennis players the best?

Novak Djokovic

3

Roger Federer

At the Match

A tennis match has a unique fan experience. During a match, it is important for fans to be quiet. This is respectful to the players. The players need to be focused. Close matches are tense. At the end of a rally, the crowd cheers!

The players love their fans. The support helps them through a long match. After matches, some players sign autographs. Some will take pictures. Many large **tournaments** also have special fan events.

Did You Know?
More than 1 million fans attended the 2024 US Open.

Rafael Nadal

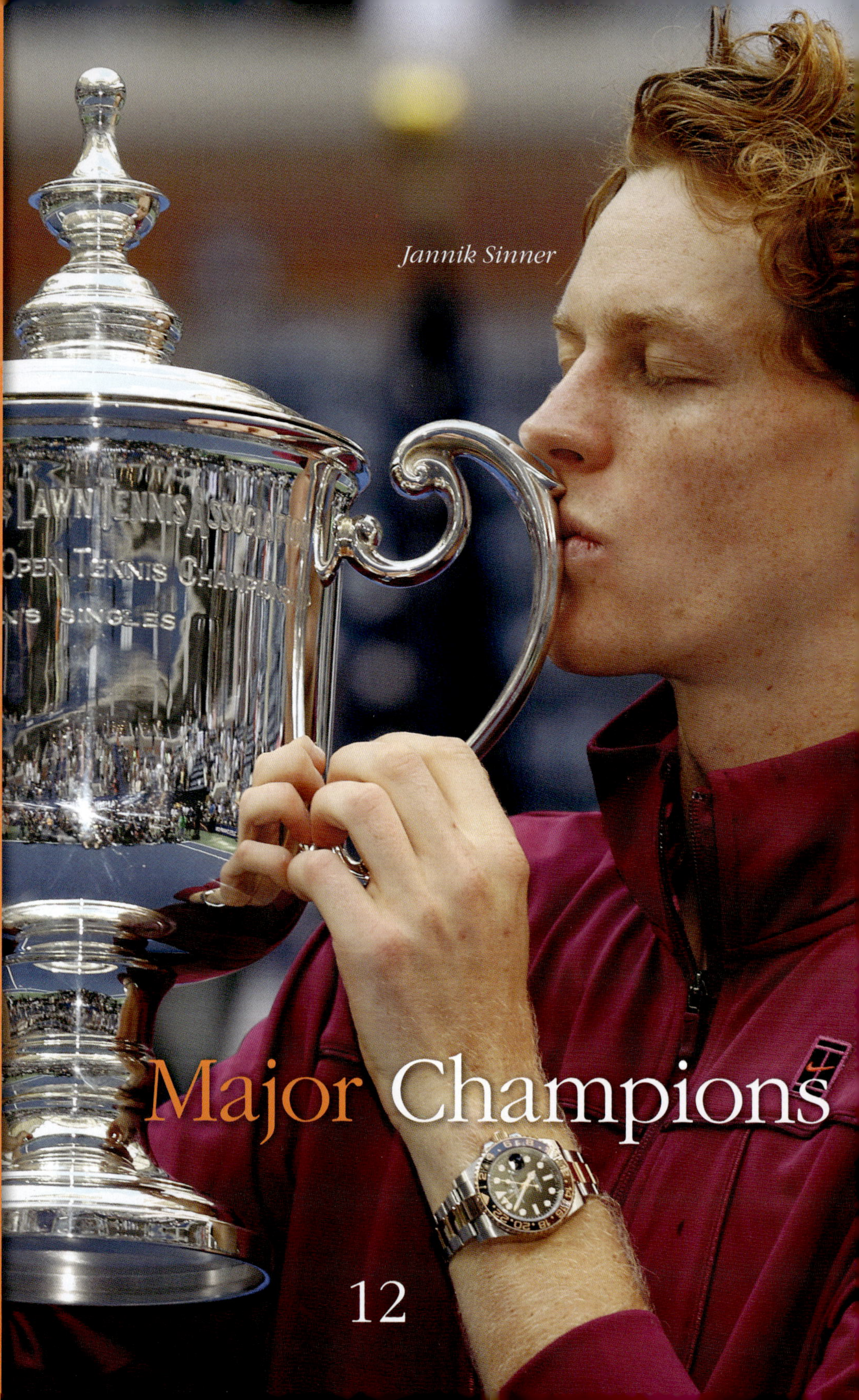

Jannik Sinner

4 Major Champions

The biggest tournaments are called majors. There are four majors every year. They are the Australian Open, French Open, Wimbledon, and US Open. Fans get extra excited for these. The majors have the most players and biggest prizes.

The majors are thrilling. There are usually many upsets. Some fans like when the underdogs win. Other fans root for the top players. The final matches are usually between tennis's best.

Did You Know?

The 2024 US Open awarded $75 million in prize money.

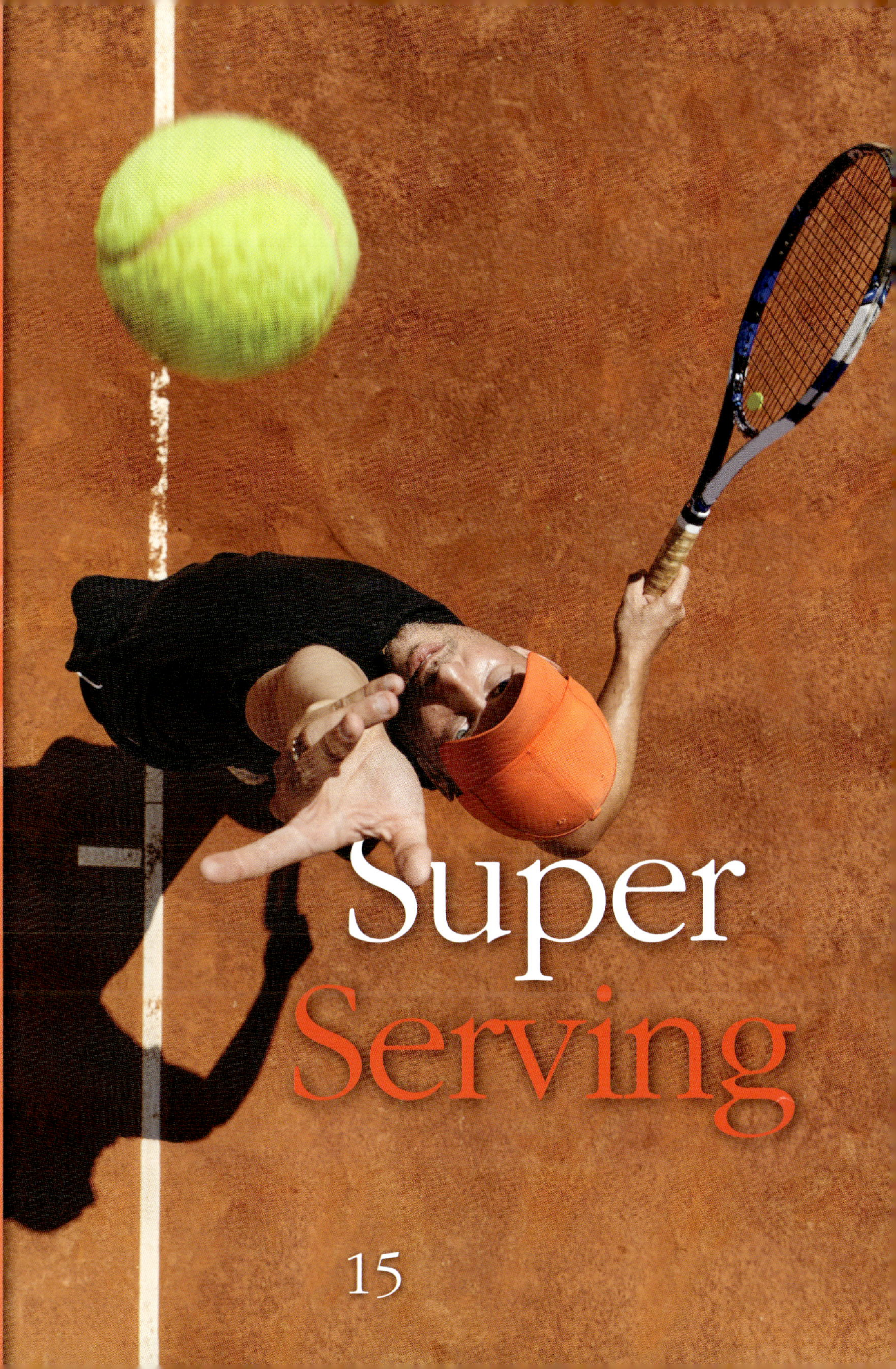

5

Super Serving

Every tennis point starts with a serve. Fans love to watch players serve as hard as possible. The crowd cheers for **aces**. There have been many great servers. Serena Williams was one. Her serve was fast and steady.

Another amazing server was John Isner. He could serve over 140 miles (225 kilometers) per hour! Other players struggled to return his serve. He has the record for most aces. Fans were amazed by his power and speed.

Serena Williams

Think About It

Do you think it is better to have a powerful serve or great returning skills?

Alexander Zverev

6

Types of Tennis

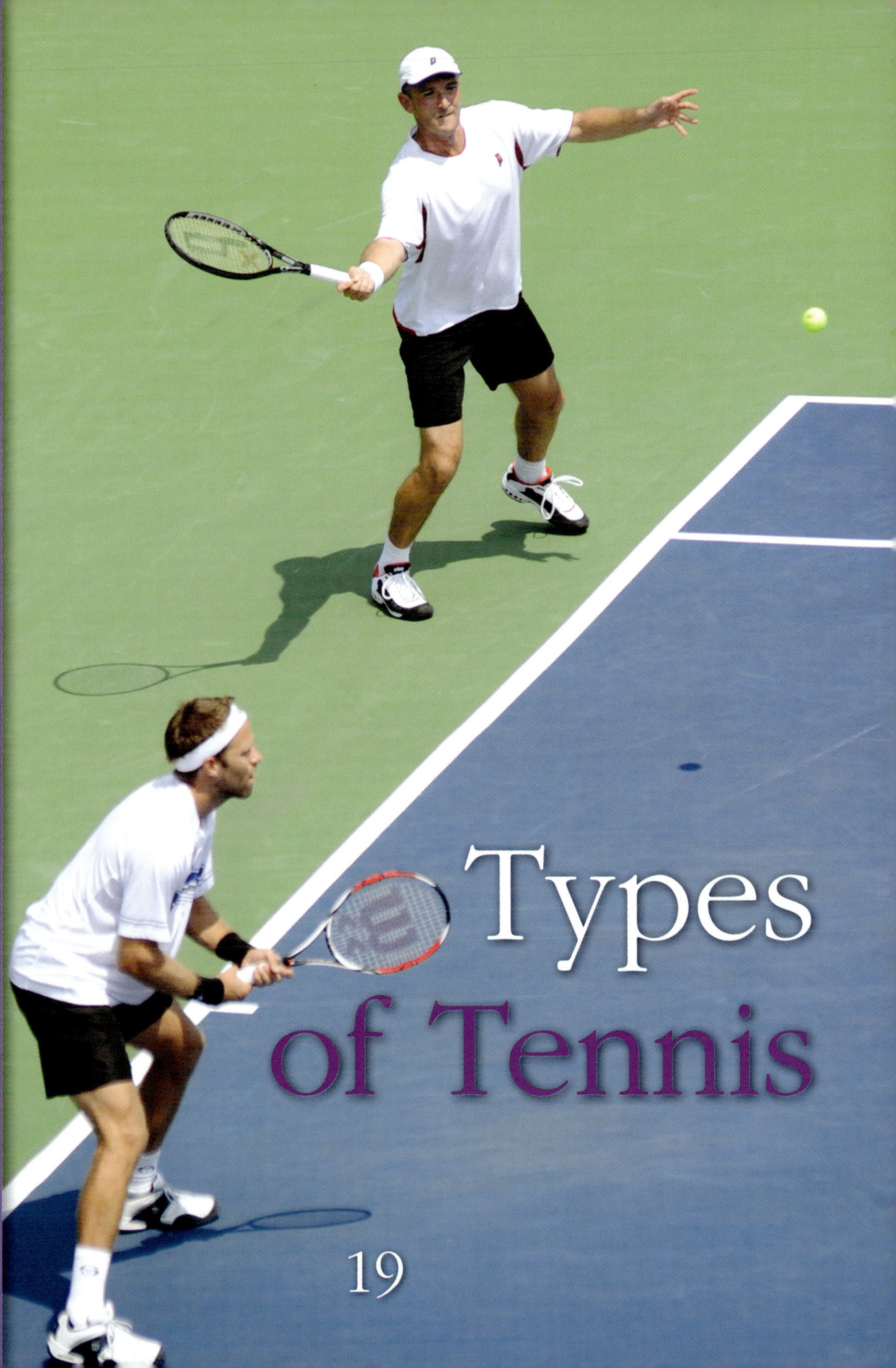

Tennis can be played in singles. This is the most common form of tennis. It can also be played with a partner. Doubles tennis is fast-paced.

Tennis also can be played on different surfaces. It is played on hard, grass, and clay courts. Different parts of the world have different courts. Players change their playing style on each court. Fans enjoy all types of tennis.

Clay court

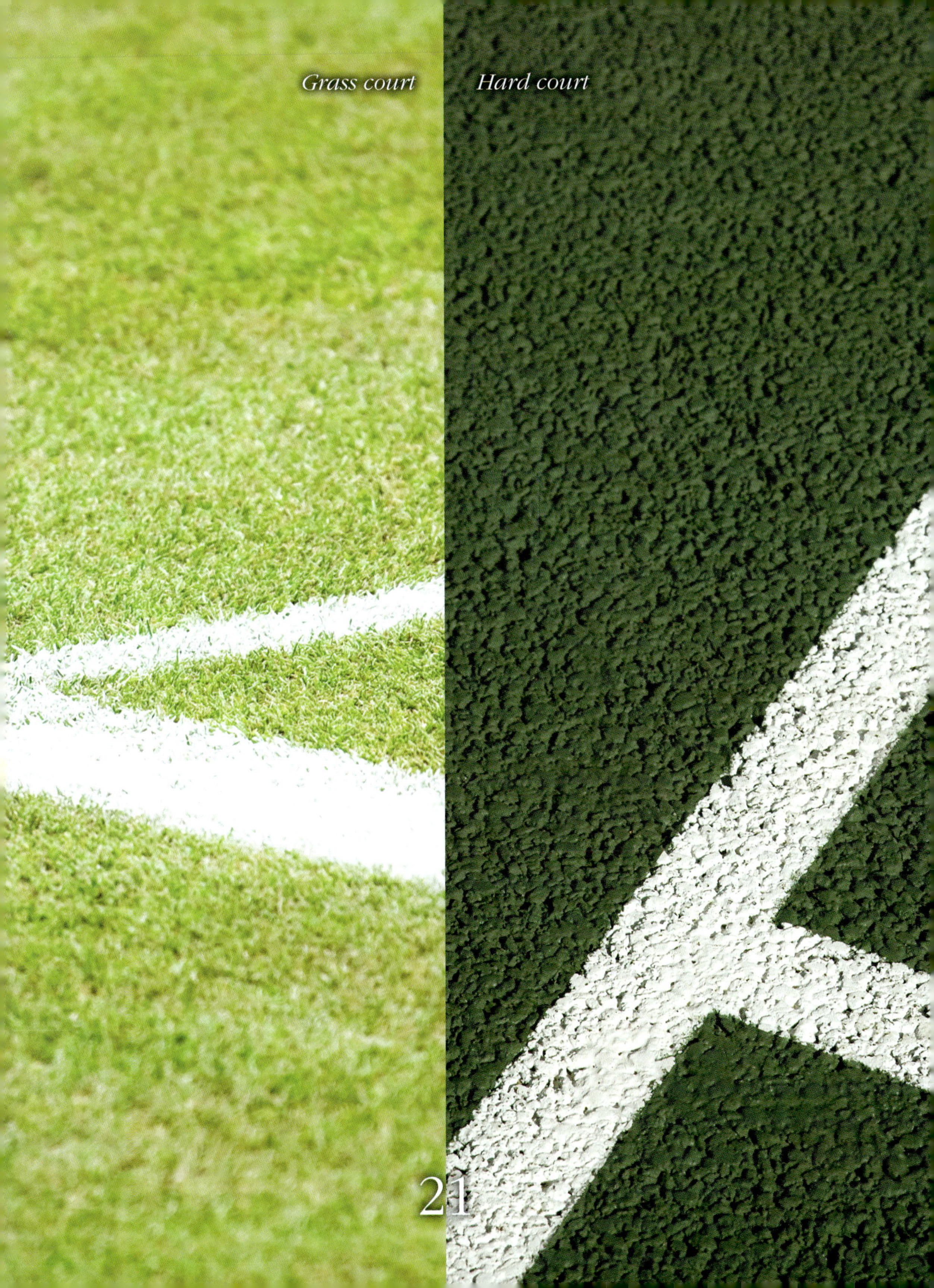
Grass court
Hard court

MORE TO EXPLORE

FANTASTIC FACTS

Tennis balls were black or white until 1972.

The longest professional tennis match took 11 hours and 5 minutes!

There are around 270,000 tennis courts in the United States.

The US Open was the first major to pay men and women equally, starting in 1973.

Only five players have won a "Calendar Grand Slam," winning all four majors in the same year.

Started in 1877, Wimbledon is the oldest tennis tournament.

MORE TO EXPLORE

COOL COMPARISONS

Which players have had the most major singles titles?

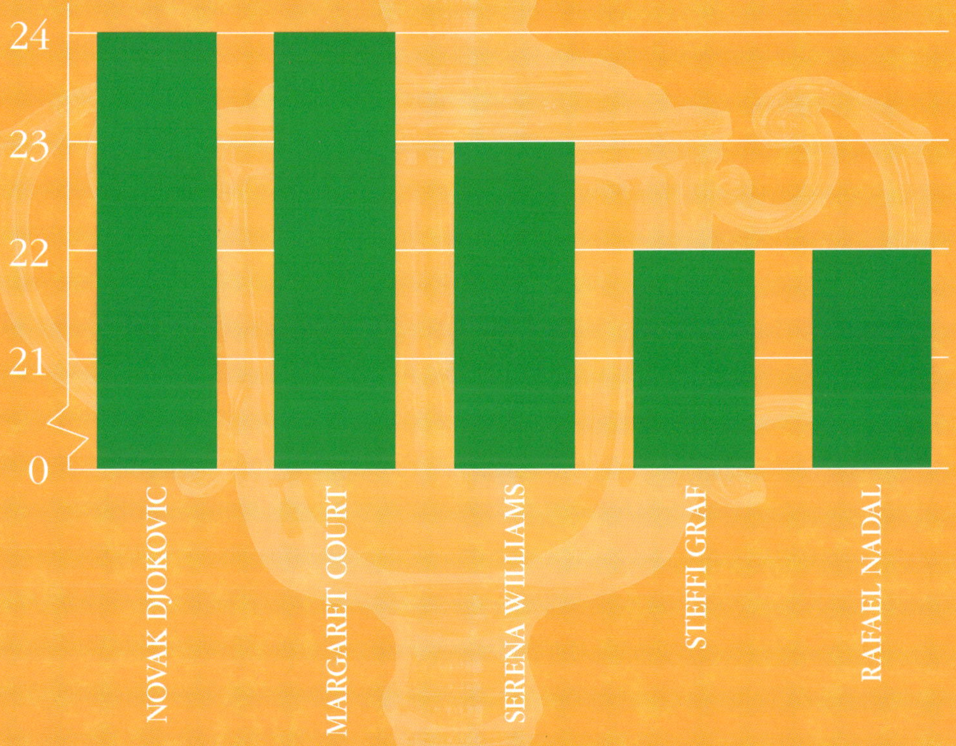

MORE TO EXPLORE

RESOURCES

Glossary

ace (EYS) A point scored on a serve that an opponent fails to hit.

dominant (DOM-uh-nuhnt) More important, powerful, or successful than all others.

GOAT A person who is excellent or the best in their field; GOAT stands for "greatest of all time."

match (MACH) A series of games played to determine a winner.

rally (RAL-ee) A continuous series of hits back and forth between players.

tournament (TUR-nuh-muhnt) A series of matches between several teams, ending in one winner.

upset (UHP-set) A contest that is won by a person or team that was expected to lose.

Read More

Blue, Tyler. *Stars of World Tennis.* New York: Abbeville Kids, 2024.

Goldstein, Margarent J. *Meet Novak Djokovic.* Minneapolis: Lerner Publications, 2025.

Index

TOP RANK is published by Black Rabbit Books, P.O. Box 227, Mankato, MN, 56002.

• Top Rank is an imprint of Black Rabbit Books. • Designed by Danny Nanos • Photographs © Alamy Stock Photo/Cal Sport Media, cover, 1; Dreamstime/Gavril Margittai, 17, Gerald T. Coli, 6, Luis Louro, 20, Paul Maguire, 21, Steve Mann, 21, Zhukovsky, 13, 23; Getty Images/Kirn Vintage Stock, 4–5, Marcelo Endelli, 2, 7, Robert Szaniszlo/NurPhoto, 18, Sarah Stier, 12–13; Shutterstock/by.LO, cover, 1, dotshock, 15, Khorzhevska, 14, Leonard Zhukovsky, 8–9, 11, nito, 5, nopparada samrhubsuk, 16, Peyker 5, Rena Schild, 19, salajean, 10 • Printed in India.

Library of Congress Cataloging-in-Publication Data: Names: Whitcomb, Aidan, author. | Title: Why we love tennis / by Aidan Whitcomb. | Description: Mankato, MN : Black Rabbit Books, 2026. | Series: Why we love sports | Includes bibliographical references and index. | Ages 8–11 | Grades 2–3 | Identifiers: LCCN 2024050020 | ISBN 9781644668092 (library binding) | ISBN 9781644668412 (paperback) | ISBN 9781644668733 (ebook) | Subjects: LCSH: Tennis—Juvenile literature. | Classification: LCC GV996.5 .W466 2026 | DDC 796.342—dc23/eng/20241129 | LC record available at https://lccn.loc.gov/2024050020